Capturing Snowflakes

Eve Pearce

CAPTURING SNOWFLAKES

New and Selected Poems

Greenheart Press

First published by Greenheart Press in 2012
Greenheart Press is an imprint of WOW Kent magazine
www.wowkent.co.uk

Design by 'A Stones Throw'
Produced by The Choir Press

A CIP record for this book
is available from the British Library

ISBN 978-0-9571829-1-2

Contents

Photograph: The author with her parents, Eva and Jack Pearce, Nice 1931

ACKNOWLEDGEMENTS

Special thanks to Susan Johns, editor par excellence

Some of the poems in 'Capturing Snowflakes' appeared in the following anthologies and publications, for which the author extends thanks: *Poetry On The Lake* (Wyvern Works 2006); *Images of Women* (Arrowhead 2006); *Well Versed* (Hearing Eye 2009); *Torriano Nights: A festschrift for John Rety* (Acumen 2009); *RADA Writes* (RADA Enterprises 2009); several editions of the *Morning Star* newspaper; *The Oldie* magazine, which published a shortened version of 'Up to a Certain Point' in May 2011. 'Birthright' was a runner-up in the Yorkshire Open Poetry Competition 2006.

The following poems also appeared in *Woman in Winter*, a 35pp pamphlet by the author published by Hearing Eye in 2007:

Birthright
Blues in the Night
Cocoon
Family Portrait
Legacy
Polyphotos
Sonnet for Dead Friends
Snowdrops
Stepmother
The English Lesson

for Millicent, Henry and Alexander

Nice – Promenade des Anglais – 1933

I remember the lizard in the street lamp,
jewel green, perfectly still.
Stamp your foot, move your head –
he's vanished. I was three.

I remember mimosa: golden balls,
essence of sunshine, scent like no other.
To be a flower lady my first ambition –
to tend a stall like the one on our corner,
to see those colours, smell that perfume
every day.

I remember the small statue of St Joseph
in the dim church, how if you placed
a centime on his tongue he swallowed it
and said *Merci*.

I remember it as a time of perfect safety,
there's a photograph to prove it –
sitting on Daddy's shoulders,
my mother standing by
in a garden full of Mediterranean sun.

Talisman

Charm held fast on left hip, shield against lowering melancholy –
all day in my pocket you've nestled, smooth oval pebble,
found above a line of glittering seaweed,
washed by waves these many centuries
on windswept Aldeburgh beach;
help me drive off the black dog
who stalks my night –
your smoothness against his jagged silhouette,
your beauty opposing his dark terrors.
But if he must stay, let me find strength
to welcome him, feel his salty muzzle on my cheek,
embrace him without fear.

The waves break once again – I shut my eyes
now wet with spray, my fingers close around you – flawless stone,
talisman in my pocket.

Knight with Falcon

He's a genius this painter.
He came to me one day in the City Chamber,
one of those interminable meetings
about God knows what, asked if I'd sit for him.
I'd seen him around of course,
knew he painted portraits.
Nobody thought that much of him.
In fact there'd been quite a rumpus
about that group he did – you know the one
where they all look pompous fools,
the worthy burghers of Amsterdam.

Anyway I said yes... *Good,* he said...
Wear your feathered hat. Bring the falcon!
And here I am. He's caught me, captured me
you might say. Amazing!
Never said six words to him, but the fellow
seems to know me. Knows I hate soldiering,
haven't many friends. Knows I love my falcon –
Titus, I call him. Funnily enough –
name of this chap's son – Titus –
think he told me he died – ten, was it?
Yes, ten... Hard that...

What I like is the way he's painted the feathers.

Legacy

for Phyllida

It must have felt a very long way
for her to come back alone,
the child heavy in her womb,
leaving behind beloved husband Jack,
knowing he'd be messing about with cars
in the morning, billiards after noon,
and as sun slowly sank into azure sea
(Matisse made manifest), the Englishman's
charm would be laid on in Harry's Bar
for the edification of the demoiselles.

It must have mattered madly
that her bairn should be true Scots-born.

Her legacy – trees, skies, mountains of this land –
the copper beech, the silver birch,
and Burns' bonny rowan tree –
these have meant much to me.
As well her Bible – tissue-thin pages
gold-tipped, faint scent of eau-de-cologne,
an inscription in her beautiful hand,
I will lift up mine eyes unto the hills.

She died when I was seven.
I remember her face on the pillow,
colourless as drifts of snow
outwith the hospital gates –

not much more. Only that when I turned
to wave goodbye she didn't see me,
had eyes for him alone.

Her legacy's been worth the telling, worth the pain,
for I have seen sunlight strike Dunottar's ruins
through curtains of rain, and wild sea-sprayed branches
cliff-high, glimpsed from a train have enlaced me
with ancient magic.

We are the things we love.

A Garden for the Gardenless

Rain runs in rivulets, sinks into sodden grass,
parched for weeks the garden welcomes rain.
At eight the bells of Holy Joe's ring out for Mass,
the faithful from Highgate Hill, from Hornsey Lane,
converge. In the Park: kids, dogs, smokers who can't stop
are running, chasing, jumping, tumbling, leaping
down to the pond, skipping, leap-frogging, hop-
scotching, hide and seeking, sometimes peeping
at the spot where Marvell wrote *his* Garden.
Will Sweet Nell appear, orange in hand, 'King's
Protestant Whore' – her own words – *O pardon*.
At Drury Lane in Covent Garden still she sings.
Waterlow, this Park, Sir Sidney gave us. Blessed
forever as "*A garden for the gardenless.*"

Snowdrops

Like the wolf in a fairy tale, biting cold
snatches at my throat as I twist the brass knob,
push the heavy door. I close it quickly,
lest my aunties hear (they've gone for *a wee lie down*).

The silence of death is in this room: Grandad's parlour,
used only for weddings, christenings and at Hogmanay.
The coffin is an alien.

Luminous light filters through drawn blinds,
snow lending opal bloom to parlour tomb.
In the polished box with gleaming handles
lies my mother.
I stand on tiptoe to see her:
white shroud pin-tucked at foot,
pearl-buttoned from waist to frilled neck,
hands crossed on breast. The air has stopped.
I've seen her, but I don't believe – I have to touch;
and so like Thomas, fearful and doubting
I lay my olive hand on her ivory fingers.
                                                        Icy.

In the forenoon I brave the slush on the iron stairs,
pick snowdrops from the back green,
wrap their stems in silver paper,
find my father, gaunt, lost – give them to him.
For Mummy – to take with her – in her hands, I say.
He nods, pauses and walks away.

I notice the hole in the sole of his shoe.

The Muse

I hoped that you would come to me today,
shyly, like a young gazelle
to one who has waited patiently
alone in the forest, scarcely breathing,
finally rewarded by the touch of a moist muzzle,
a huge eye so close to his he drowns in limpid black.
But that is not what happened.

I thought you might come without warning,
as they say love does occasionally,
minds and bodies fitting together perfectly,
the heavenly plan falling into place
to the strain of celestial choirs.
But even though I played it very cool,
you didn't show.

I thought I might hear hooves thundering –
in dream perhaps – and there you'd be
on your white charger, scarlet cloak billowing,
sweeping me up with a glorious shriek,
doubts dispelled, inspiration descending,
never to retreat, never to retreat,
never to retreat again.
It didn't happen. You didn't come.

I gave up, then, having found you – Muse,
inspiration or whatever –
as difficult to come by as a lover;
not to be pinned down, not the butterfly
dead on the page –
more the bird who swoops and glides
hanging on to the wind's tail.

At last I started off without you,
crossing fingers, trusting you might
drop by and without a word
breathe on me one day.

Strange Relationship

I celebrate you, old rectangular block of wood
found this morning discarded on a bench.
How beautiful you are!

I see the bark of your ancient parent tree,
rough to the touch, smelling of forests long gone;
you have a personality – I can tell.

Someone has knocked nails into you –
the holes have become your eyes,
and you are watching me.

I love the tiny oval ring etched near your base.
To touch you is to send shivers up my spine.
As soon as I set eyes on you, I felt a connection.

I have even dared to taste you;
bitter with a touch of sweetness.
Now we are mingled – now we are one.

Cocoon

Numbing, freezing, this December day;
breath visible in the foggy air
tastes metallic on the tongue.

She's close to me today – my childhood self –
thin seven year old struggling with scratchy socks,
garters so tight they leave a livid band
of skeleton white below the knee.
Swollen fingers squeeze shiny chilblained toes,
purple and itchy, into harsh brown brogues.

Today I'm seeing her plain –
brown eyes like almonds, straggly fringe,
a wee thing in her too large prickly coat
made by Granny overnight and black as the grate.

Safe in my grown-up bed I still
can hear the treadle's song:
wha'll care fir ye noo yer mammy's deed,
wha'll care fir the mitherless quine?

On February mornings, on her way to school,
she's capturing snowflakes, white lozenges
on her tongue: standing still, head tipped back,
great flakes falling on eyes and lashes,
nose and lips – a world of snow
swirling and spiralling about her
as she prepares to enter her silent cocoon –
black changing so slowly to white.

NB: 'Quine' is the word for a girl child in Aberdeen

In the Same Country, Shepherds

A cold crisp night it was,
a thousand stars in a sky you could drown in.
We were lying on the hillside resting,
the three of us, the other twa half my age.
Hearing the swish of his wings (like chainmail
mair than feathers), petrified we were.
The lads telt me he said *Fear not.*
Why then did I hear *Dinnae be feart,*
the words my faither used when some horror
shook my childish world? *Dinnae be feart.* Aye.

Of a sudden the sky was full of angels
singing *Tidings of great joy –*
born this day a Saviour – Christ the Lord –
ye'll find him wrapped in swaddling clothes,
lying in a manger. Weel, swaddling claes,
common enough that, but *lying in a manger –*
a manger! In a byre? Wi' the beasts?

Still we kent we had tae go, even if something
telt me oor lives wad niver be the same.
Oor quiet life, smell of wool on damp nights,
baas of the ewes afore the newborn's bleat
said the struggle was over and we'd won.
The peace of a windless starry night –
never mair! The ithers didnae want tae move
but I kent weel we were privileged –
commanded by angels, no less.

So aff we went, and right enough we found him
in a manger; a peely-wally wee thing –
his maither nae mair'n a quine.
I bowed ma heid, the ithers did the same.
I pit doon the lamb I was carryin' –
it went straight tae the babby and licked his face,
so I left it as a wee present.

I'm the only yin left.
Baith the young yins died within five years,
so I'm left tae tell the tale – only tae folk
that ask, ye ken, aye, fewer ivery year,
and less wha credit it.

One of these days there'll be naebuddy.

Debbie Dancing

She's fifteen, blonde curls flying,
essence of joy, of youth,
existing only in the moment,
Debbie, to the strains of *Angie Baby*
dancing her heart out.

Thirty years have passed. I'm on a train
from King's Cross going to her funeral.
Found in her flat in York; nobody knows
how long she'd lain there. I hope
the drink worked and she never woke.

Life was not kind to 'Angie baby',
the same age as my own daughter,
but for me she will always be
the girl who never stops dancing.

It could be yesterday –
the shabby school hall, light catching
the golden hair, the pop song,
and Debbie,
Debbie dancing.

Green

Green are the forests – green the fields,
green the frogs newly painted,
green the 'gages bought in case of hunger.
Green your eyes which the visor shields
from overbearing sun.

In their cages the tigers crouch, panthers stalk.
State of the art this, you know, the Keeper boasts,
a pyramid of stages where you and they –
the animals – can walk,
the dignity of both preserved.

The Northern Lights had a great swathe of green,
a satin cloak flung into lowering sky
the night my childhood ended.

I note the flash of green in the eye of the tiger.

Last Year of Peace

I'd walked up Holborn,
turned into Union Street.
Sentinels – the clocks of Remembrance
began to chime the hour,
not all in perfect time,
but perfectly attuned to the moment:
the eleventh hour of the eleventh day
of the eleventh month.
At the first chime people stopped,
men doffed their hats and all stood still.
And so did I. The year was 1938.

That was the last year I spent with my father.
We slept in the big brass bed in our one room –
no mother now between us, I curled round his back,
so warm and soncie and safe.
I didn't know he hated the cold granite,
the wee wifie's gossip behind lace curtains:
Puir wee mithirless quine – he's English ye ken!
There was no work. Depression reigned,
the dole money kept us in a manner
to which he was not accustomed.

School holidays were spent in the Billiard Hall.
The owner felt sorry for him, a widower left
wi' a wee lass. He spoke French, they called him Froggie.
Gies a bitte French, Froggie.
Coloured balls held in their triangle,
deep dusty fringe on green-shaded lights.

I chalked cues, kept score,
kneeling up on torn red velvet seat
to reach the brass tally board above.
The only child allowed – Heaven!

Summer evenings would see us at the Dog Track
beyond the Bridge of Dee, his charm loosed
on the turnstile girl. Oh what a charmer!
We'd get in for nothing at half-time.
A penny to bet on the oilcloth.
You choose the dogs, Bunty, you're the lucky one.
A gambler never stops, even when the stake's a penny.
So our last year was shared between Dogs and Billiards.

One Sunday in September I came home
to find him listening to Mr Chamberlain –
you know the speech – and he was smiling.
War, he said. *Daddy will have to go, you know.*
Why? I asked. *To fight Hitler,* was the reply,
and he couldn't seem to stop grinning.
Next morning he was first in the queue to volunteer –
his escape – at last.

The Hawthorn Tree

O I remember the hawthorn tree
and how its blossoms pink and white
gladdened my lone heart and set it free.

Many magic things there were to see,
I was a child and all was full of light
and I remember the hawthorn tree.

Arms once were eager to envelop me.
I see him – my body leaps – the sight
gladdens my lone heart and sets it free.

Ah! Now I come home to joyless tea.
Daddy has to go, he says, *to fight.*
Yes, I remember the hawthorn tree.

The tree's thorns prick. How can such things be?
You love me. Do not go! Hold me tight,
gladden my lone heart and set it free.

Too young to know then why he had to flee,
war his one hope; I couldn't sense his plight,
but I remember how the hawthorn tree
gladdened my lone heart and set it free.

The Stones at Coole

Sometimes on autumn evenings
the house seems to whisper, the stones speak:
I have been beautiful in my time –

and am still lovely for those with eyes to see;
honoured too, before his terrible beauty,
by one who'd seen the breasts, white
as driven snow, of the wild swans at Coole,
and thought my pristine stone, pure Portland,
virginal, my windows facing stormy seas,
seeming to ride the waves as swans the lake,
meet for his pen to celebrate.

Now year by year a little more is lost
from the crumbling cliffs – I feel them shift,
I hear them grate and growl.
Tiny pebbles, showers of gravel
will be my undoing.

Like traitors, now remembered only
for the fine men they betrayed.

I have been beautiful in my time.

Birthright

Aberdeen! Jute Street – fifty-five. *Aye, right.*
Are granite slabs still split in mason's yard? BOOM!
the giant hammer swings. I shiver with delight.

Memorials for Aberdonians, angel-bright
marble monuments defying endless doom.
Fifty-five Jute Street – here y'are, and I alight.

Back green – iron stair. I'm six, leap the last flight
to suck on rusty fleur-de-lys, taste of the tomb
floods my mouth now. I shiver with delight.

Patterned lino on inside stair – no light
but on heavy door brass plate gleams through gloom.
Fifty-five Jute Street, Aberdeen – this night.

Granny's speciality was the bear-hug *Tight.*
Brawny arms surround me. Safe as in the womb
I gasp for air and shiver with delight.

It's why I came. In cold North-Eastern light
would memories, sae lang syne still bloom?
Fifty-five Jute Street Aberdeen is my birthright.
I was born here. I shiver with delight.

Poem for John

April is not the cruellest month,
    Eliot was wrong.
For me it is always February,
    February all along.
A short month, the stiletto in its mouth
hidden by snow (and there is always snow),
waiting for that certain day –
my mother died on that day,
years later my husband's mother too,
on that same day, the sixth day.

And you, dear John, how was it that I didn't learn
until that certain day that you had gone
three days before, and all was changed?

Eliot has a Game of Chess.
Is it possible you still might play?
I see you shake your head – no.
But after all is said and done
we can only guess whether it be bright day
or endless night beyond that bourne from which
no traveller returns.

The best that we can do is keep your world,
as we have understood it, imperfectly, like children
in our hearts and in our verse
as long
      as long,
          as long as we shall live.

He Called his House Highwood

I didn't like him – that's the first thing to say,
he didn't expect to like me – why should he –
not only an actress but a divorcée,
wanting to marry his only son. But Lily smiled.
Lots of tonic, I said, when the G &T appeared.

He called his house Highwood – name of the copse
which in 1916 changed hands twelve times,
eight thousand men perished, and tanks were used
for the first time; great lumbering iron beasts,
and he was in one of them. No air, stuck in mud,
a sitting target. I knew his story, but took no heed:
Now I want to tell it.

He came back, married Lily, who bore him one child,
a son. *Why only one*? I asked, years later.
Joe didn't want any more, she whispered,
looking round to make sure he couldn't hear.
Said son was sent to boarding school in Wales
when he was seven, *To save him from the bombs.*
Bombs in Marple, Cheshire? Surely not!

One day, pointing at his son, he told me,
You've no idea what a trial he was to me.
How, father? I asked. *He cried,* was the answer.

His own father used to stand outside the cotton mill,
gold Hunter in hand, waiting for it to strike the hour –
seven, or was it eight? Men who turned up late
given their cards on the spot. I think Joe would
have liked to do that, but times change.

He had to be content with pettier tyrannies:
warning me never to use all three bars on the tiny
electric fire in our freezing bedroom (I did once
and fused the whole house); limiting phone calls,
convinced they'd bankrupt him; insisting on
Bird's Custard when they came to dinner with us.
To this day I hate the yellow gloop.

When Lily died of a sudden heart attack
he became a broken man, so vulnerable.
She had been the mirror through which
he saw himself. He shrank visibly –
maybe the terrors of the Somme moved closer.
Who knows? At any rate he became a lost soul.
Did he wonder why he had been spared
to join a world which had not seen the things that he had seen?
Did he dream of young men,
friend and foe, bodies twisted together,
severed limbs protruding from the mud,
fanned by leafless trees in that copse,
that Hell, called Highwood?

Back home, how could he tell Lily, or his sister Olive,
or anybody who hadn't been there, of those things?

When he bought his house, a large one
above a sloping garden, with four trees
standing together,
he did the only thing he could:
he called his house Highwood.

Stepmother

She was very small,
she always wore black,
she was not in mourning
for her life or anybody else's.
And I loved her.

Straight of back, elegant of foot,
a tiny wildcat fearing nothing;
offering the startled burglar a cup of tea,
though white hot Irish temper flared
alarmingly at cruel words or deeds.

She was a champion of pitiful things –
bones begged from the butcher
for a one-eyed, mangy mutt,
smelly sprats boiled up for the alley cat,
and the child that was me rescued
from festering boredom in a cold city –
shown a world undreamed of:
London seen through pillars of white,
lime juice and cheese straws to eat,
a soft divan to sleep on.

Most mornings, even now, fifty years on
I wake expecting her for breakfast:
coffee, croissants, cherry jam –
till I remember with a tiny pang
she left me years ago.

My Life in Shoes

Two years old – bare-toed sandals in Mediterranean sun.
At four, Wellington boots plough through Scottish snow.
Seven brings mourning black patent for Mummy.
New brogues travel to London at twelve.
High-heeled straw sandals herald maturity.
Navy blue marriage suedes promise too much.
Principal Boy – satin heels with fishnets.
Low heels for pregnancy – three times:
happiness – despair, a seesaw, so many shoes.
Old now, fear falling – non-slips, low with Velcro bar.

Family Portrait

Grandad, you're pickled in aspic –
I can't get through to you.

Sae lang since, a hundred years lang syne
you sat for the family portrait,
you and Stewart and Granny – mine,
but one I never knew, though having her look
(or so it was said) when I was a quine.

Fine she still sits in her velvet black,
wee lassie on her knee,
angled away, lost in thought, a knack
you laughed at – aye a dreamer she.
Two years, two more bairns before she's laid
in lonely grave.

Aged two, my Auntie Elsie, heather-filled basket
dangling from tiny fist, frowns at a world
which soon will leave her crippled, a misfit.
Bored nursemaid, steep brae, pram overturns –
bonny blue-eyed lass, white dress, blue sash,
rendered into the fearsome maiden aunt I knew.

You're pickled in aspic Grandad
as you pose in your Sunday best,
your braw wee lad perched on velvet chair,
in his hands a tall wooden ship, and lest
he will not part with it, cannot bear,
you let him ken – in your gentle voice:

It's nay yours, Stewart, just haud it for noo.
So he gives it back to the photo-man
when the last flash dies, just as he would one day
fight in Flanders, in his unquestioning, obedient way.

My Uncle Stewart, who one fine morn,
having delivered the daily milk to Maryhill
let himself in, noticing his sock was torn,
leaving his Wellingtons like sentinels
outwith the door – saw the water how
it sparkled, filling the green enamel bowl –
socks off, and careful not to spill now
on gleaming lino, stepped in, sole
arbiter at last of his own destiny – his life –
holding a chrome electric one-bar fire,
(bought recently to please a strong-willed wife),
leant to switch it on, and deep in the mud and mire
of Flanders – smelling the stench, hearing the guns,
finally joined his pals, a few years late –
poppies bursting in the air like scarlet suns.

Mona Lisa

I remember her eyes, the pallor of her cheek.
  Everyone says her smile is memorable,
    but imagine prising open the crate,
      shining my torch on her and
        she looking straight
          at me,
          at me
        poor gangly Hans.
    Fit to freeze the blood that night,
   but this flame was leaping inside me,
  my breast like burning coals – she spoke –
whispered *ich liebe dich*. I dropped the lid and fled.

Next night we went back, treading like Wenceslas' page
  in one another's footsteps, no lieutenant to stop us.
    The plan: to move the Nazi bombs, all eight
      into the belly of the mine,
        far from the treasures.
          Sweating
          I was
        all night, thinking
      of her skin, her sideways glance,
    the secret smile to drive a man stark mad,
  twice I thought I heard a whisper, then laughter.
Three times I opened my mouth to tell. She stopped me.

A few days later it was over. The Americans showed up,
couldn't believe their eyes... Headlines screamed
LOOTED TREASURES IN SALT MINE.
We were heroes, all five of us
for a week and a day.
By then
I knew
who she was, but Paris
said no. She'd not left the Louvre
the whole of the war! I could've told them!
Ach nein... But I'll tell my son the tale before I die:
La Giaconda smiled at your Papa: whispered *ich liebe dich.*

*From 1943-1945 the Germans moved thousands of works of art, looted
from all over Europe, to the safety of a disused salt mine in the Austrian
Alps - Altausee. When it was obvious that he was losing the war Hitler
ordered the Gauleiter of the region to place eight huge bombs there.
The treasures were to be blown up, rather than have them fall into
Allied hands. However, the official in charge of Altausee, Emmarich
Pochmuller, decided this was a bad thing, and on his orders the bombs
were moved away on the night of 3rd and 4th May by five common
Austrian soldiers.*

Polyphotos

Taken soon after I arrived in London –
one polyphoto from a sheet – thirty
I think – an inch square, in black and white –
this the sole survivor.
I was twelve and longed to see the new me!

Pat, indulgent with the waif she'd acquired
along with a husband – said Selfridges
was the place, so we walked down Edgware Road
and I was immortalised on Selfridge Lower Ground.
It was 1941.

Here I am, biting my lip slightly,
but happy with my sprigged blouse,
my brown skirt with straps – height of fashion –
ribbon (I think it was red) a bit skew-whiff
in my hair, my dark eyes full of hope.

Polyphotos had conquered Europe too
it seems, in the midst of other conquests –
your Diary has a page of snaps
and there you are, an Amsterdam version,
looking up at me, dressed not unlike,
with your black hair, your beautiful dark eyes.
The year is 1941.

My heart judders, as the trains must have.

I've always known: we could have changed places.
Only seven weeks separate us.
Look at us – expectancy in our faces.
We are like two stretches of smooth sand
the tide has not yet reached.
When it does, you will be swept away,
I remain safe for sixty years.

Brave my sister, stay a little longer,
and when I need it, hold out your hand
and help me through the dark.

Remembrance Sunday 2011

I'm standing by the window,
London a deco carpet at my feet,
all squares and triangles.
11 o'clock – Boom! – and the city holds its breath.
White roses on my balcony are still in full bloom.

Sun low in the sky
producing crisp shadows
like Mondrian shapes
as the Queen steps backwards
into shade, and bows her head.
A beautiful day – a gift of a day.

Later, on a bus, the man who looks like a tramp
chooses to sit beside me.
He's carrying his filthy plimsolls,
his feet battered and bloody.
I say, *You should get those seen to.*
He says, *I remember the holocaust.*

I want to say, *So do I,* but the words
disappear like ectoplasm, even while
I'm forming them. Your man gets up,
swaying from side to side,
making for the back of the bus.
The driver pulls over, opens his cab,
shouts, *Sit down, will ye?*

I know what's coming. As if in reply,
I remember the holocaust,
he pronounces, quite quietly, not emphatic,
just that it's on his mind, and needs to be said.
But he sits. The driver is pacified and we go on.

In the evening - at the going down of the sun
and at home again, I think of my Uncle Stewart
who survived the Somme
but needed to join his comrades
and claim a blood red poppy for himself –
and one fine day, did just that.

The Spinster's Song

How many times have I stood here
on this desolate corner waiting?
Sometimes there's been a shard of fear –
still and ever I've stayed here – anticipating.

On this desolate corner waiting
for love I suppose you'd have to say.
Still and ever I've stayed here – anticipating,
and this could be the day, my lovely day.

For love, I suppose you'd have to say –
One fine day... one day my prince will come,
and this could be the day, my lovely day.
Dreams fulfilled, wishes granted. Sound the drum.

One fine day... One day my prince will come
in sun, rain, snow, frost, gale or even hail –
dreams fulfilled, wishes granted. Sound the drum.
It cannot now, dear God, it cannot fail.

How fast they go, the unintended years,
on some occasions there's been fear.
My hair is white. My sunken eyes drop tears.
How many times have I stood here?

Three O'Clock in the Morning

I dreamed of you again
Federico Garcia Lorca.
As always a scent of roses
came before you appeared
on a white horse, a garland round her neck,
her flanks drenched with sweat.
Federico Garcia Lorca
why do you come to me?
Can I stop the bullet in the field?

Your eyes as they look into mine
are bewildered – you were in a safe house,
the house of your friend – a Falangist
but still a friend: his mother took you in.
The Black Squad came nonetheless –
oh yes, nonetheless
Federico Garcia Lorca –
your talent your undoing.

In the morning the sun shone,
the Alhambra sparkled,
and they shot you *with several others,*
buried you in the ravine where you fell.

Why do you come to me?
My heart leaps. Your white horse –
Ah! The passion in that horse –
she rears and whinnies.
The scent of roses fills the night.

Federico Garcia Lorca
I shall dream of you again.

Andromache's Lullaby

Today you are anchored to my belly,
and I am rocking you, cradling you,
your fine gold hair on my shoulder,
a scarf of grief.
They will come soon to take you away,
to dash you from the highest rock –
we all know the place, overlooking Troy.

I don't want to do this says the Greek herald.
He looks kind. I believe him.
No doubt he has children of his own.

The women are keening, beating their breasts.
No words come to me, no tears.
I rock you my son, my only son –
Hector's child – golden one.

Sleep now my love, so that the moment
when they snatch you from me
may be as a dream, and you wake only
to a flash of blue.

I am rocking you now,
rocking and praying to Zeus,
to Hera, Queen of Heaven –
such a little boy –
to add you to her family.

The Herald says it is time.
My arms tighten round you.
I bless your astonished eyes,
bluer than the skies above.

I call your name:
I let you go.

The Ring

Thanks for that lovely present,
my beautiful ring –
bluest of blue enamel,
diamonds blinking, winking
(at the joke perhaps?), all set in gold,
an old enchanted thing, your final gift –
my haunted beautiful ring.

Of course it's what I asked for, that last Christmas.
(Much to your surprise).
A ring! you said, but straight went out and bought it.
(Much to mine).

So thanks a million! I shall treasure it –
as well as our three children –
your parting gift, salve for a broken heart.
And I shall wear and cherish its cold beauty
long after you have gone –
gone to another wife, another life,
twelve thousand miles from us,
on the far, far other side of dawn.

Sonnet for Dead Friends

Twenty five years since she swallowed the pills,
gulped the brandy, kicked off her scarlet mules,
waited for sun-drenched death in Beverley Hills:
long-limbed, life-loving Rachel, breaker of rules
felled by life's blows: a careless man, no child.
Then Roy – graceful, spiky, gifted, gay –
his heart gave way: Larry – warm, beguiled
by beauty, caught an eternal cold one day.
Marion, so young – Teddy, so frightened –
Glen, dearest of all – we sang to you,
hoping you heard, trusting the songs lightened
your heart, as rose sky turned to deepest blue.
They are gone – I remain. Death's a game of chance;
a leaf blowing in the wind, for them I dance.

Longer than Love

My first love Jimmy wore maroon,
a corduroy jacket – easy to fall for,
given he was tall and handsome,
and I all of seventeen.
Add Chekhov – I *was* that Seagull,
and you've got a match.
Love seemed to beckon – how was one to know
except by trying? (Like Sylvia and Ted).
So after we agreed to join his choir
Dr Soper married us in Kingsway Hall.

Then I learned what love was not.
Jimmy did too I suppose,
dancing now to a different tune,
she, with her Yma Sumac voice
the star act in Astor's night club
in Berkeley Square. No nightingale.
Still he had eyes only for her.
Shall we dance? and left me at the table
without a glance. I was hurt – incredulous,
but his friend, the boy with the red-gold hair
won't stop talking. *Look at me, not him,*
he seems to say. Passion streams from him –
football, for Heaven's sake! Man. United,
you've guessed it. Eventually he worked his magic,
offered to take me home.

Sixty years on, and he's long gone
to a wife who doesn't do football.
But I have three great children, the last a strawberry blonde,
and now a granddaughter with that same hair (genes are odd)
born to the dark-haired sister.

It's rare I miss a match when United play,
mostly on the tele now of course.

The beautiful game, it seems,
lasts longer than love.

My Friends the Crows

Every year they come – this the fourth –
the same pair, I'm certain.
Even February snow doesn't deter them –
still bitter cold, but when it's time, it's time.
One day I hear a caw, then another.

High up in the great horse-chestnut,
branches covered in snow, spring cleaning begins.
One lands – hovers – lands again –
his own personal trampoline.
Last year's branches are discarded; the other
brings fresh twigs, honed and bent to shape.
A few weeks and it's finished.
Now only one crow swoops over my balcony,
berries in beak, food for his mate
sitting on her eggs.

One beautiful morning,
silhouette against a cobalt sky, I see
the tiny open beaks, heads back, hungry –
but that was last year.

Two weeks' sun this year means I've lost them.
Overnight, leaves appear, then candles.
The male still swoops over me:
the nest is hidden in green shade.

I won't see the young until they fly.

Song of the Blues

Last night I swam in tears,
sinking in our boat-like bed,
our gondola you called it –
found you'd taken the pole.

In the end the whisky worked.
I slept – woke in tomb-like silence,
that hour between three and four,
true middle of the night.

Legs feel for other legs
turning in a slow pavane.
Realisation dawns – wet blanket
flung on shivering body.

Mouth cracked, lips dry
I get up, pass long mirror in the hall,
try not to see this apology for a woman;
mouth open - a scream with no sound.

Creep back to cheerless bed
clutching my faded blue hot bottle,
to lie, slipping in and out of sleep
until a dawn as pink and blue as litmus paper.

Up to a Certain Point

I remember the first time I saw an evening game under
floodlights. It was at Bolton, and the Wanderers were
playing Man. United. I remember climbing the iron
steps, stopping at the top, looking down, and the grass
was this dazzling green.

I remember Bobby Charlton's goal from miles over
the half-way line – just after the Munich crash.

I remember Keith who was to be my second husband
wooing me with his passion for United – I who knew
nothing about football mesmerised by this boy with
the red-gold hair.

I remember knitting my lovely lacy red jumper.

I remember my first pair of high heels – straw
embroidered sandals, with flowers on them, and red
cords around the ankle.

I remember the taste of sherbet fizzers in a yellow roll,
sucked through a liquorice stick.

I remember black and white "strippit balls" that lasted
for ages if you sucked them slowly.

I remember walking to school up Broomhill Road
through four foot of snow.

I remember "slides" in the playground, made on a
slope, by dozens of boys' shoes going back and forth
until the surface was like glass.

I remember the boys' faces, but not their names.

I remember Elsie McDonald, with whom I vied for "top of the class", and Jean Forrest, whose mother liked me, and who had a board on which you stuck bits of coloured felt to make pictures.

I remember Eunice Donaldson, whose mother was English and who lived just round the corner. She was my best friend and had a mop of lanky fair hair.

I remember seeing all of Shirley Temple's films by myself in the afternoons, and how I loved her golden curls.

I remember seeing the ushers at the Capitol standing in line for inspection in the foyer before the cinema opened, and how they had to hold out their hands, palms up, then down, to show that their white gloves were clean.

I remember jumping with terror when the Wicked Queen in Snow White first appeared as the Witch offering Snow White the poisoned apple.

I remember I was so terrified of the huge white marble statue of the old Queen Victoria, just inside the Music Hall, that I hid under my mother's skirt – and later when I came to London I didn't like Madame Tussaud's, and I still don't care for indoor Sculpture. There was a huge white marble eagle in the Aberdeen Art Gallery with wings outstretched. It seemed to fill the entire width of the room. That was a real nightmare for me.

I remember how cold my mother was when I crept into Grandad's parlour, where she was lying in her coffin and touched her hands; then her face... Icy.

I remember the gilt clock on the mantelpiece, with a handsome young man in breeches and open shirt, lying on the ground, holding up the face. The numerals were in delicate gold. But the little gold balls which went round and back were not moving, and there was no sound of the minutes ticking away, because the clock had stopped.

I remember the smell of vinegar from the saucer under the coffin.

I remember vinegar soaking through the newspaper when you bought a fish supper and ate it on the way home.

I remember hating having to pose for a photo in the Fish Market, holding a dead cod by its gaping mouth.

I remember the smell and the dreadful taste and texture of Scott's Emulsion, which I had to take every morning, because I was supposed to be delicate. It was made from Cod Liver Oil, and was very thick and very, very white.

I remember the lizard in the lampost in Nice – how green he was – how still he was when still – how fast he moved when disturbed.

I remember a small statue of St. Joseph in the dimness of the local church. His tongue protruded, and if you put a centime on it he nodded and swallowed it, and said *merci*.

I remember wanting to have a white dress with a
veil for First Communion, and being told I couldn't
because we weren't Catholic.

I remember in the Gospel Hall in Aberdeen, where
I went to Sunday School, *because it's the nearest*,
there was only one piece of decoration, and that was
a scroll on the wall above the platform which said

GOD IS LOVE
John.iv.8

I remember Miss Ingram who was my Sunday
School teacher wore her beautiful ash-blonde hair
in a coil round her head because female Brethren
weren't allowed to cut their hair.

I remember being invited to tea at Miss Ingram's
house on the Sunday after my mother died, and
given special permission to do a jigsaw by her
brother, the Superintendent. Normally children
were forbidden to play on Sunday because it was the
Lord's Day. The jigsaw showed Jesus on a Donkey
entering Jerusalem on Palm Sunday.

I remember my mother in a long blue velvet dress
with pearl buttons, reciting 'The Queen's Marie' at
Aunty Peggy's wedding, and everybody clapping
like mad. I suppose they knew she was well on her
way to death. But I didn't.

I remember the peach crepe dress Granny made
for me to wear at Aunty Peggy's wedding. I had a
velvet band round my head with artificial flowers on
it, and ribbons down the back, and I had to carry a
posy in a doily, because I was the Flower Girl.

I remember the doll's house Uncle Charlie made for
me. It had a light powered by a battery in the roof,
and this was a wondrous thing, because our room
was lit only by one gas mantle.

I remember the hiss of gas when the mantle broke.

I remember the street lamp outside our room, and
how it made the mica in the granite shine, especially
when it rained.

I remember it was raining the night I saw a photo
in the *Press and Journal* of the King on horseback,
and my Daddy told me he might have to abdicate. I
didn't know what that meant, but Daddy explained
that he might not be King any more, because he
loved an American lady, called Wallis Simpson who
had been married before.

I remember waving my Daddy goodbye on Aberdeen
Station. He was wearing his new khaki uniform with
the buttons all shiny, and was going to a camp called
Catterick. He said he'd send me a photo from there.
And he did.

I remember how excited I was when Pat, who had
been a friend of Mummy and Daddy in Nice, asked
me down to London for a holiday. The journey took
16 hours, all through the night. I was twelve and fell

asleep on a soldier's shoulder, and he didn't dare to move. Daddy met me at King's Cross, and we caught a red bus straight away and sat on top in front, so Daddy could show me London.

I remember the house where Pat lived was in Clifton Gardens. It had white pillars and a balcony on the first floor. Pat said the pillars were called stucco. I thought they were beautiful.

I remember Pat who was Irish, had made cheese straws and served them with Rose's lime juice. She said it absolutely had to be Rose's.

I remember Pat shouting to me in the bathroom, *I don't hear much washing going on.* I was just lying in the bath, because it was the first proper bath I had ever seen. But you could only have four inches of water because of the War.

I remember when Daddy and Pat got married in a Registry Office on the Harrow Road, I heard a woman onlooker say *Fancy getting married in black!* But Pat always wore black, and for this occasion she had chosen a little black dress with gold embroidery. She said it was *très chic.* And it was.

I remember my first day at Parliament Hill School. Smetana's 'My Homeland' was playing on a gramophone, and there was a pear tree in full bloom outside. I sat next to Esmé and fell in love with her golden plaits.

I remember Esmé being expelled, and going to St Martin's School of Art, because Art was the only thing she wanted to do, and she refused to work at anything else.

I remember my first wedding to Jimmy in Kingsway Hall, and Dr Donald Soper, a famous Methodist preacher agreeing to marry us if we joined his choir. So we did, and Esmé designed my hat.

I remember the first time I saw Keith all I noticed about him was his strawberry blonde hair. He had managed to borrow his father's car, and drove us all out to the Ribble Valley – Jimmy, Herbert, Jimmy's Cairn terrier Ruch, and me.

I remember my first night-club and how upset I was because Jimmy hadn't asked me to dance; instead he was dancing with Joan Turner, the star of the show. Keith and I were left at the table, and he started wooing me with his passion for Manchester United – determined to get my attention away from the dancing pair. In the end he managed it, and took me home.

I remember seeing Pelé play in the Final of the World Cup in Stockholm in 1958. Keith was covering it for the Manchester Evening Chronicle, and I went too. Pelé was 17, and Brazil won!

I remember that somebody opened a small gate at half-time and I found myself in the Royal Enclosure. Keith of course was in the Press Box. Offered a glass of champagne from a silver tray it seemed churlish to refuse!

I remember Keith asking *Where the hell were you? You were supposed to meet me in the bar at half-time.* And my reply, *Oh I was drinking champagne with the King of Sweden.*

Inspiration

One thing I know, one thing –
when I write my sermon I am inspired,
God is in me, I'm certain of it –
He comes down like the cloud
that hovered over Moses and his people
in Sinai, in the desert.

My mind is the desert. The cloud brings rain,
manna too. He feedeth me. He leadeth me
beside waters far from still.
My cup – my cup – my cup runneth over
runneth over with ecstasy
as the Holy Spirit swoops –
no dove – an eagle, a Roman eagle.
Tramp of centurions' feet, deafening.
I cry out, *God, my God,*
wake, clutching my sermon,
damp, dank with my sweat.

Porridge before church. I need my strength.
I shall deliver the Word of God.

Twenty faces look up,
blank as empty notebooks.
I give my sermon, my gift from Him,
His revelation. No one is moved.
No one is changed.
I shake the inert hands, I smile,
enquire politely after absent friends.

Six nights to go before I am inspired again.

The Dog Days

Sirius is high in the sky and bright –
the Dog Days are upon us,
those days when even love must twice
be summoned – the firmament too light
for secrets – and what is love out in the open
for all to see?

Every living creature feels the heat,
apathy overcomes desire. Dogs famously lie panting,
tongues lolling – any patch of shade becomes desirable.
Involuntary sleep overtakes the lover
and his love.

We didn't know – didn't care about the Dog Days –
we were young – bathed in sweat our love
was consummated – with a hey and a ho
and a hey, nonny no.
Marriage the key we thought – chose the fourteenth of July-
Bastille Day – Liberté, Egalité, Fraternité,
such triumphant symbols.

Funny how we never thought of the red caps,
the clatter of tumbrils, tricoteuses knitting on
as heads rolled. Maybe the Dog Days kept us
from thinking overmuch.

Not till years later did the Dog Days strike.
A girl – twenty years younger than me –
our three children made no odds –
the Dog Days were upon us once again,
And in the Southern Hemisphere Sirius shone bright.

Breathe into Me

Shall we go, you and I,
to where those mountains draped with snow,
like the bare shoulders of women
seen through flimsy Shetland shawls,
loom from the mist, or slam upon the sight
sudden against a sombre sky.

Here, soft rain will wash us clean.
Stay still and let our bodies mingle;
breathe deep, breathe into me, into the hills
till we and they are one.

Soon the snow will reach us,
soft blanket cover glistening limbs.
We shall become as ice,
frozen in love that will endure.

Larry's Funeral

Thirty we were, roughly that,
more than I thought would come.
Still-lovely sister Gloria, erstwhile dancer,
in unbrushed black, leaning on her only son
beloved Marco – standing when the rest of us sat down:
far from Florence now, each body-movement
seeming to ask: *What now?*
I never thought I'd have to play this role,
I left this country forty years ago
when even entrechats were easy.

The coffin was borne in, set gently down.
No music. He'd wanted silence – a Quaker funeral.

His father, a French Jew who ran a successful business
importing fruit and veg, was proud of the belt he'd won
for amateur boxing – his photograph
with arms raised in classic pose had pride of place
in his small flat in Newman Street.
We stayed there once when he was away.
I had quite a shock on finding a huge revolver
under the mattress next morning.

Larry so different – an actor, handsome in his youth,
loved art, collected a little, learned gilding,
my Victorian mirror shows his skill.
You've got the picture, have you? You haven't!
How about spying for the British in Egypt –
still refusing to talk about it years later?
One day he ventured, *I'm reading the Bible.*
All of it? I said. *I think so – yes, it's good!*

Yes, I said, feeling strangely honoured that
he'd trusted me with even that much.

A private man was Larry,
a private man was he,
I loved him like a brother
and I think that he loved me.

The English Lesson

A hand held up, a hand with a small hole:
the autumn sun, dying like mighty Caesar
shines through – halo of gold on pallid palm.

A small man, Mr Maltby, suited in rusty navy,
striped shirt with collar not so much frayed
as chewed. *This afternoon*, he says – *Shakespeare*.

A sort of sigh goes up – the dusty air
charged with anticipation. Of what?
Today, he says, *I give you Anthony.*
And he holds up his hand.

Friends Romans Countrymen –
No need to ask us *lend our ears*, or eyes,
that one translucent spot everyone's focus.
Then I remember, cornered at playtime,
being told – *bullet went straight thru 'is 'and,*
'e told us once – 'strue – 'e said it wor
a place called Passion Dale.

So Shakespeare's murdered Julius
fell for us on Flanders Fields, and in light
of setting sun Caesar's corpse was strewn
with blood-red poppies.

Now Mr Maltby becomes the noble Roman,
no longer bald but crowned with laurel,
a full length robe – the toga suited him –

best of all the small hole in his right palm
convinced us that he had seen War,
Betrayal, Death, and earned his right to move us
with Shakespeare's words – we, the unlikely mob
at Caesar's funeral.

Into the Bright Moon

Light strikes in front of my bed.
Shards of frost glimmer.
I lift my head to gaze into the bright moon;
When I lower it, I see the place where I was born.

Lang Tae Wait

Weel, ancient I may be, bit a Granny.
I'd lang tae wait, thocht it wud nivir cum,
bit life's a funny thing, ye cannae
tell when it'll deal a body blow, or sum
wee pressie – jist when ye'd gied up hope
and thocht ye wernae fit; and ye'd better be,
for Grannies are aye on call; so dinnae mope,
be a'ready fur the crisis, bit see
ye're nae mouthin' the borin' platitude:
aye weel, this is the way I used tae dae it.
The wurld his changed, ditch that attitude,
zip up yir lips, or hoo's yir dotter tae dae it?
Jist ask the guid Lord tae gie ye a few
mair years, 'nd whiles tae bless the bairnie too.

Playing Statues

I see now we were playing Statues,
an old game with a new twist.
He moved so stealthily, with such speed,
light on his feet – dancing almost –
I was never able to catch Him in the act,
taking my fingers from my eyes
and looking round reluctantly.

Only the smallest change in you, beloved friend,
signalled His silent move – your head grown heavier
ceased to fall awkward to one side, now
never moved at all. The little treats to tempt you,
tomatoes the size of marbles, tiny grapes –
one day your mouth stayed stubbornly closed.
He'd done a pirouette and struck an attitude.

Soon after He pointed at your poor parched lips,
from then on you were dumb.
Only once we heard a high, thin sound,
animal it seemed, not human:
unforgettable.

I knew that He had almost won,
but love does not give up so easily.
We sang your favourite songs and hymns,
anything we remembered, our eyes so full
He could have made His last move then and there
and we would scarce have known.

In the early hours, they said. So I hope
He took you, who loved dancing, in his arms
for one last dance before He let you go.
He is, after all, only the Messenger.

Blues in the Night

I love musicians –
the way they simply pick up their instruments
and play.

Jools Holland – lovely Jools, had a very old hand on
the other night: Dr John. Must have been
doing his thing *since Pussy was a cat.*

The Doctor wore a green felt hat
with a brighter green ribbon round it.
His suit had seen better days.
The baby grand had a strip of coarse lace
tacked on to the straight bit – a human skull
sat on top of the piano. Nobody
said a word about it. It was just there.
Memento mori with a vengeance.

Gravelly voice singing *Blues in the Night.*
I'm seven again, sitting at my cousin Freddie's feet,
and he's belting out in a Glasgow twang –
Ma mama dun tol' me, when I was in knee-pants,
Ma mama dun tol' me son – a woman's
a two-faced, a worrisome thing
that leads you to sing
those Blues in the Night.

We got *That Old Black Magic* after that.

I love musicians.

Small Things

The winter jasmine is early this year,
November dusk at half-past four
is pierced by pale yellow stars,
tiny flowers braving sleet, braving gales,
harbingers of spring in autumn,
delicate blooms which lighten mood,
lift depression.

Noah's dove – how frail she must have seemed
pitched against endless waters, a small thing
chosen to fulfil a covenant,
and not till the third try was the leaf found,
the promise fulfilled.

A daisy in his hands, Rabbie Burns looks
over the railway tracks in my home city,
sad that he's trodden on her loveliness:
Wee, modest, crimson-tipped flow'r
Thou's met me in an evil hoor.

Of course we yearn for fame,
to cut a dash and win a medal,
to be recognised for our achievements.

But what shall I remember,
what shall I recall
when dusk falls for the last time?
Maybe these tiny points of light
will pierce the gloom, and I shall say,
the winter jasmine is early this year.

9780957182912